The Flammable Bird

For
Charles
where all beginnings
start aflame!
Ignited,
Elena

The Flammable Bird

Elena Karina Byrne

Zoo Press

Zoo Press • P.O. Box 22990 • Lincoln, Nebraska 68542
Printed in the United States of America

Distributed to the trade by The University of Nebraska Press
Lincoln, Nebraska 68588 • www.nebraskapress.unl.edu

Cover art, *The Flammable Bird*, by Elena Karina Byrne © 2002

Cover design by LeAnn Jensen © 2002

Library of Congress Cataloging-in-Publication Data

Byrne, Elena Karina.
The flammable bird / by Elena Karina Byrne.— 1st ed.
p. cm.
ISBN 0-9708177-8-9 (alk. paper)
I. Title.
PS3602.Y76 F58 2002
811'.6—dc21

2002012445

zoo010

First Edition

Acknowledgments

Grateful acknowledgment is made to the following periodicals, in which these poems originally appeared, sometimes in slightly different form:

The American Poetry Review: "Breaking Unbalance"; *The Antioch Review*: "Every Definitive in July"; *The Colorado Review*: "The Proportion of Broken" and "Mutiny Allegory"; *Denver Quarterly*: "Kierkegaard Knows No Shame" and "Liberty As Warning"; *Greensboro Review*: "Portrait Under Stress"; *Jacaranda Review*: "Thirst For Them"; *Nimrod*: "Porcelain"; *The Ohio Review*: "Magritte's Hat"; *The Paris Review*: "Sanctuary of Hunger"; *Ploughshares*: "Remote"; *Poetry*: "In Particular"; *Pool*: "Red"; *Potpourri*: "Nothing is Anonymous"; *Quarterly West*: "Darwin's Window"; *Salt Hill Review*: "Ghost: A Love Story"; *Virginia Quarterly Review*: "Immaculate Measure" and "Without the Elation of Rage"; *Volt*: "Entrance of Flowers".

I would like to express my deep gratitude for my parents, Herbert Samuel Jepson and Marcia Shlaudeman Jepson who supported me always. Unending thanks to my lifelong "Don," Thomas Lux, my friends in heart and mind, Cathy Colman, Doreen Gildroy, Galway Kinnell, David St. John and Sherod Santos.

Special thanks, for their support, to pals Henry Mansfield, Zach Hinchliffe, Jeffrey McDaniel, Carol Muske-Dukes, Judith Taylor, Molly Bendall, Karen Sexton-Josephs, Rex Wilder, Giorgio Baroni, and Bill Wadsworth. An inspired thanks goes to those who were there at the start of it all: Judith O'Hanlon, Esteban Cacícedo, Donald Bell, Timothy Dansdill, Kathy Kamel, David Phelps, Lisa Terenzio Meade, Sheila Gray Baghdad, and Merlin Bolton-Smith.

To the heavens, ignited love and gratitude: Agha Shahid Ali, Doris Curran, Ken Nelson, my father.

All of me and what's left of me, to my husband, Peter James Byrne.

for my Dylan James and Chloe Karina

Table of Contents

I: The Flammable Bird

Sanctuary of Hunger 3
The Proportion of Broken 5
Nothing Is Anonymous 6
A Portrait under Stress 7
Sleep in Your Birthday Suit 9
Window Portrait 11
When Words Fail in the Body 12
Porcelain 13
Ghost: A Love Story 14
Entrance of Flowers 16

II: In Particular

Remote 19
Kierkegaard Knows No Shame 20
Origin of Bees 21
Darwin's Window 24
Mother Tongue 25
In the Kingdom of Beetles 28
Animalia 30
Paul Klee, Inexact Diaries 32
Magritte's Hat 33
God's Watch 35
In Particular 36
Answering Machine 37
Liberty As Warning 39

III: The Indignance of the Future

Pig's Eye 43
Immaculate Measure 44
Without the Elation of Rage 45
Thirst for Them 47
Breaking Unbalance 48
Childhood 51
Without Exception 52
Every Definitive in July 54
Mutiny Allegory 55
Of Angels & Loneliness 56
Bee's Connubial Hive 58
Red Pillow 59
Red 61
Palm 62
To Bird 63
Watermark 64
The Future Comes to Him, Faithless: A Dialogue 66

IV: Lost Vernacular

Copernican Revision: The Flammable Bird 69
Detail in Black 70
Field of Aphasia 71
Going after Shakespeare 72

Notes 74

I

I do not know myself, and god forbid that I should.
—Goethe

Sanctuary of Hunger

Give her this goodbye, give her no destiny in desire. No matter
what she knows, it's not enough. The limit of hunger within her blooms

and blooms. The pit in the stomach shines. Measuring the world
as a place to hunger after, she shapes its taste in her mind, squeezes

berries till they bleed down her arms, kindles her umbrella fire
until it swarms words back up at her. She cannot get it

to her mouth fast enough. She cannot stop herself. What rush
correspondence of blood replenishes dangerous wish—what deepens

umbilical will? There's no stopping it, no one to stop it. As she curls in
on herself, she is certain longing is a link to breathing. Always returning

to the farewell feast she fattens on for the future, hunger drops
the perfumed orange bait down into the water. The water rises to her

tongue. But she is thirsty as anguish, reminded there is no safe place
to go to, no common ground here, so she pays close attention to abandon

and the body. If you let it, real desire can rise out of anything: bone, whole
fruit, green along the ground, October with its giddy confusion of color

and the sure asylum sweating-out dream. But this *necessary irrepressible*
will always be interrupted and there is no mind-map where we choose to perish.

The uphill climb eventually leads to a new home. Look, look where she comes:
even the dirt is hungry. She knows what to feed on: she grazes the flowers ahead

of her, face down, smells and polishes the gourd of gratitude. Let her create
something new out of the lost old, create from the open bowl of black ink.

This is the well water run underground and beneath sleep. Well-spring
of self, the lost and found for thinking. Let fault of what is missing, desire

from her now. With the devotion of starving, let her be the deep water wish,
exile of flying. She will awake the excess of summer inside her, until delight

weakens her appearance. Placing its inevitable purpose upon her, she will find
the sanctuary always changing. She will go there with all she has.

She will go there hungry, but she will not eat.

The Proportion of Broken

When time is broke and no proportion kept!
—Shakespeare

Relentless, I love relentless: relentless
doors and windows unhinged with their ways to open.
Thinking that cannot stop or
that bee-hurry, honey-havoc hive.
Some simple cogs and wheels;
something is always on.
Live sea that cannot stop
breathing, dog chasing its scrap tail, red bird
at the wind, always one flying
from the sky's china arms. Chatter, ants, television.
I know no place like it. Relentless Earth
and no other way out. Incoherent
as seed and as close to the ground. Someone will come
to dig there with relentless tenderness.
Flowers, in their relentless kept beauty, will wait.
There, disembodied as doubt,
the fog will double in, even try to convince
itself indebted blind, of its own way.
To outdo any word of mouth or maintenance of mind
the dream keeps relentless time.
Dreams keep relentless white air for you to breathe
and without any hope
of departure, they keep the love that will strike its blue match
over and against your heart without bearing broken
from one world to the next. I sleep
out of this inconsolable chaos,
without a roof where there is no proportion
kept, until troubling the abrupt reeled-in hour,
I alone might appear as a matter of fiction
for this relentless will to forever have and have
me again, till it has me, to hold.

Nothing Is Anonymous

No fallen tree, misshapen
cloud or the sky's underwater mirror,
elation's incandescent new lawn before spring. Even

our names before they were given to us: not anonymous.
Entropy's sweet chaos
had a hand in someone's life, personal once.

Cursive arrows, the Kingfisher's feathers
or El Greco's blackest ink and a blade
of grass, a blade of silence on the tongue.
Ecosystem and cycle, ghosts

of trash from the street float
in the ocean. We walk out into a room
and belong. Someone's perfume
floats down a staircase long after they're gone.

The computer's windy voice, telephone's
hollow: not without he or she
having their way with you.

It's all the same, so what "I", what itinerant
click of the universe sends us packing
from anonymous? You can't get around it.

I pack my suitcase, I rest
my case. There are people
far lonelier than I.

A Portrait under Stress

I have cornered myself away from matches and mirrors
Because lately, when I loom in their field of displaced light

There's this woman wearing bare disbelief and a bee headdress: master,
Transparent will. She is filled with unthinkable lust, salt

Water, and oil paint. She won't look me in the eye for long and stares
Just above the mirror's yellow envelope like a bare, blind bird

Then resurrects a farewell smile, prescient before leaving.
She cannot wear roses. The roses, cannibals, wait in the abstract

Garden of hunger and love. Adumbrated haste, blatant patience.
There's a pealed error of recognition when she sleeps,
an occupant-voice

That calls out from the zoo inside. She begins every day without me.
She worries too, when I'm not there, lets the animals out.

Fish swim from her breathing, morning birds call, all
Animals, body parts move in translation. Without hope, she can't

Even remember jokes, is certain she's going to die
When on a roller coaster, but allegorical, on a good day

Without numbers, her mouth knows the equations of grace:
Kiss waking apart, undressed. Look and look

Behind the intoxicant-dance, the last dark remembering
Dark from her horizon here. On a nervous continent

Separating from its deep earth-shelf, she sees herself on the tip
Of the tongue of happiness and in the manna garden

Hanging out the wings, tacking up the vines, murmuring flames
And shapes of fruit. What fat chance, what undone music.

What could I have that she could want so badly? She
Wears my clothes and returns to the recurring world outside.

She knows where I live. By circumference, she knows my name.

Sleep in Your Birthday Suit

Ring the pseudonym. Wear the mask.
It is your face to stand above
        the wooden totem pole. Like all
the babies you know, squeaky clean, multiplying
the odds like blue stars on water.

Let yourself be solvent as licked snow.
This guise, a flesh fit for any use.
        You are bearer of gifts
and lost names. Take your time, take
the pink medicine of hope on the tongue.

Each hour will taste of you
        then. Each minute will empty
its glass into you. But what does that matter?
You are home to no one. You are

the lost letter taped to the black back
of a mirror. This is
        your memory. This is
your skin and bone-halo in the dark,
the ghost of distraction you gave up.

You have nothing else but what is lost
        and gained by your own making. Don't worry,
I have you in my sights: indelible mark, birthright,
an image in the eye of your own storm.

I'm like you, thirty nine years
to the occasion and ready for it. Don't be afraid.
        What is insatiable is sweet. Faithful
whetstone and blade. Faithful stopping place, profane
garden. The botanical doctor will

make house calls. Green will be edible
          on occasions like these. You will know
when there are secrets you cannot contain.
Queenship, nothing has been taken from you yet.
Forget nothing. Dream

you are not alone, there. Less than
the company you keep, you are as sure as due
          North. Now. Leave all the windows open.
There is hope. I can see it, as if I entered the light,
for the last time, incandescent, in your eyes.

Window Portrait

Not at first: you don't see the face.
You don't see the fine Japanese paper visage, someone
you knew at the back of the brain once, certainly
someone as familiar as an exhale: winter's first ghost.

The green beyond her is illuminated now—green, taking
over the look of the yard
and if you keep staring out of focus
that face, especially the eye,
sees through you, knows your lack of time, knows
your lack of sense, how hard it is to speak
to one another from this place
of glass disappearance, and sees through to you, the face

so abstract
in the window, headless and bodiless
as if seeming to be real, right there
where it belongs, as if
it will always be there with you when you
press your shoulder against the hard transparency-cold,
though not your cheek
and its oil-wing,—but by apparition, if alone,

you knew what to do with yourself,
in time's window, for yourself, and if too,
desire were a part of recognition, then, and only then
would you wake up to examine
from the crowded weeds and gladiola stalks, your face
with its kind disinterest and row of eyelashes,
almost human and hovering
with its singular brown eye, looking back,
looking out for you.

When Words Fail in the Body

You reach under the bed,
untie the wisteria vine
of your tongue
from each spring, loosen
the stuffed, mindless cotton
from its one
white industrial embrace: safe
you climb down, slide
under the body of yourself
imprisoned above, face-down
onto the cold-knuckled
floor, Plato-naked,
the thrown metal jacks of the past
balanced on the back
of each knee, atop the coccyx
and deep in the nape,—there, breathe. Now
you are poised for the dead

for your father's mathematical grasp
of eternity: radiant, between
blinding neon and fluorescence,
where the infallible religion
of elevator music floats overhead
just to confuse you more.
But you can rearrange the syllables
of *mother* and *doctor*, throw
tomatoes and bruised fruit
at the door marked *future*.

You can keep yourself
down for the count and with a kind
of vernacular inattention, hear something
familiar, legible as the body
or your entire family,
and press one ear back to the block of mattress
until: silence
like cigarette ash, deep
as empty space.

Porcelain

Here is my everyday earthenware:
My French, my Italian origins
Universal map, the shell you put to your ear
        hearing the underwater unconscious fold of the sea
Where these lips of indiscretion open

Indefensible flames' lips, fire within the hive,—here is
My plum and pit fallen to the dirt
My pink cowrie curl where you never finish your pretext
My whereabouts, inner architecture or the fine china placed at
            your table

        and at your devour
Diminutive name claimed by no one under invitation
        of tongue and finger bowl, sweet
Ware bestowed by extravagance and skin

My belonging, my forgetting, every distinction of sex
Pig language and Latin where premise is flesh
        and the porcelain bone is raised to the light, to the lips
        of the next man who admits to me, he is not just what he
            has learned.

Ghost: A Love Story

Words are created by error. One
kind of these is called ghost words.
—Bill Bryson, *The Mother Tongue*

I. Consonant and Vowel

Consonant occludes with his hard *d, b, t, p*
and obstructs what he can with *v, z, s,*
all the while with *m* and *n* diverting her.
Too willing to be alone and self-sufficient by *a* and *e*, vowel will
still ransom and run by his side, though usually slow
in her ache and swoon, in her *o*.
She takes him to task,
breathes easily from proof to pomegranate, moon
and cum; she opens her bright bud
in the groin. Even against
the violence of his harsh wish to be known, she belongs.
So, he waits in deep exile with her,
                                        with all that has happened
or unretrievable, with all that will occur in the future,
a phantom command at his heart.

II. Object

In the bright blood of now
they will cast their fishing lines for
a portion of heart and flesh,
                                        they will split the difference twice
between them. She will walk into the green
sea over her head until it holds her breath for her
and that night, with the practice of disappearance
she will sleep, her hair, a fallen object
scattering black grains of sand on the pillow
while all along he will push them both toward the bright end.
But there is something not all together gone,
                                        in their mouths, just beginning.

III. Ghost Argument

She follows geography, an angel
that peels paint from houses, fires that ride
the wind's heave and hurl into another hill, another
seed brush and eventually to another house.
She beds with birds and water.
There are wings that make the same shapes
as the sounds from her mouth. There are sounds
that have feathers,
                                        heart-wind, weightless

bird departures across a vast ink-blue map
rendering the return of navigation
and there might be a confusion:
other bodies and other birds that hold
onto the light. But she will believe
her body back into his
and without the ability to lie, retrieve
only air.

Entrance of Flowers

No road to get there, not even the rhododendron
which sounds like road at dusk. No road angst. She will walk
up the mountain, her body gathering green as she goes by, this
new green of stopped breath
drawing her in when she reaches the top
to the skunk weed field where lemon lilies are resilient
to darkness. The cold there will tighten
like a man's grip under her skirt, a certain
vertigo-pull toward her belly's center where fear
falls confused with pleasure.
As if reversed in becoming, she stares and forgets
how to speak. She will shrink
as the flowers seem to grow and brighten: flesh, phalanx, flower.
Her lips will open as if mouth meant *net*
to catch tiny silver-thin fish of last light.
Now, history's flower-curved abstract
has her. Now, the milkman's clock
will break in the bottle of sky, its milk beads
of bird song rise to a vast dissolve,—all air
will turn taut as a clothesline swinging its clean blue
sheets above her, in that same final blue
color from the eyes of her dying father
and the first color she will remember
when at last rewarded back
to living, she walks out
into the open, the entrance of flowers.

II

Silence is a prophecy.
—Susan Sontag

Remote

How far, how far would it seem, ahead of the body?
Remote takes its time, taciturn.

Spool and furl, hope's quick unravel—remote:
a royal worth of dead watches. Replaced

hour, single shade, the white-put-there, polite winter,
strange chance. Remote turns pale and sends us away

to the next abstracted space where Remote's relatives live
in a remote village. Dreaming ahead of oneself.

Pace from refuge, irresistible: take the bright sting in love
remote cannot give because, distracted by nature, remote is remittent

and therefore not to be trusted. It cannot rage or chain-smoke
in the dark. These dull habits, careless words from our mouths,

with their indiscreet destination: Remote.
Political religion, riches, a simple way out.

There's the feeling of great loss in these things, what
can't be here, kept at an arm's length.

By purpose, abandoned numbers know their argument
of the soul and the weakness in being alone. Remote. What

distance can surmount the small odds of two bodies in the world?
Insufficient as the burden thought: Remote, one, Remote, two

Kierkegaard Knows No Shame

Anxiety is the dizziness
of freedom.
—Kierkegaard

My names have no faith. No birds. No marriage
without revelation. I have walked with this dizziness,
with the anxiety of seeing myself.
Liberty gives no warning.

I was told Kierkegaard
took long walks with God
in his head. Whether by accident or the will
of one thing, Kierkegaard knew no better.
He knew no hazard-blue way.
He could throw the dice
of logic every day over his shoulder
and come clean again.

Religion takes on science:
star-drunk, deferred forlorn light.
My backyard shares some of this
salty religion but there's no green evidence
now, that anyone ever walked here with him.
No conciliatory directions. No
field glasses, no compass.

Take a chance, I say to myself,
you are alone in the guise of burning,
in another declared country
with a fling of seeds, fallen dare.
The sky breaks open there and you garden in
with the smell of yellow pears
on your skin. Freedom knows no shame.

Shame knows no Kierkegaard, either.

Origin of Bees

Go back to the Irish beach, a bee, beech, the tree
And its papery first writings kept scratched, dry and drawn-in
Like bees' wings lining our lungs.
History has it down: a bee in the bonnet
Works at it and works hard.
Apoplectic pollinators
For the edacious future of flowers.
I slip my tongue into their flute-throats
And leave it there for the dizzy incoherence
Of bees, —Fields
Full of them, full of the honey
And harmless, domesticated sweet or
Bumble and stingless, killer and drove, and really
Wordless, seemingly blind
        As Huber the Swiss naturalist who knew them well was.

Mellifluous
For the first time, as if
For the first time you groomed the compulsion here
On the page, slaughtered the ox
And split his carcass wide, my carcass
To spring from both our sides
The spontaneous combustion of bees, Orphean and looking back,
Spreading out into the Cyclamen sky, flames
Of them rushing out as words, knit-black
In their sting of origin, so many of them I cannot count, cannot
Count on them. But wrench me anyway, startle me
From this Eclogue engine. Pull me from the umbra breast,
Let me write this: what
        Propagates the self from the self?

By chance
Their fabric is now fate, listen hard enough
To their drowsy lumps of sound, their savage speech
Catching fire. Breathe, breathe in deep
To tell yourself; just try to catch up, carry their crepuscular torch, keep

Their diurnal trail ahead of you.
Nourishing inversion,
Throw out the linguistic hand-me down logic and
Boom an imitative word to land on your feet.
I bloom everything here yearned for
            From the ground up.

Bees—in defiance, I swallow whole, dust
Of their bodies, yellow on my lips
To outlive the bee-dance, break the providence of doubt
And cross the threshold again and again, cross pollinate. . .listen
Hard: these sounds take liberty,
Release in all directions toward
A circular dwelling, self-devouring country of falling.
These sounds, this homecoming, campanion-home
And instrumental hive
Has me. I will drown in its light, play ghost to God
And tip the scales. Fever-pulse always finds change.
So I clench my teeth tight on their wax
Their verse, and this
Made mead I drink—it is thick.
I drink it with a piece of beebread
For this conversion from silence. For a little taste
            Of the bee's knees inside. Delight

Is a bewildering in the body, the life and death
Of bees spun from the origins of poetry. I cover my ears there
Thinking they will enter me, foraging passwords
In the form of scent from the dancer's mouth. 'Round dance' 'Wagging dance'
Telling direction.
Bee woman by chance. See,
The dark leaves me now and I am as bright as new love.
Can our inclination fall toward farewell
            Before we find our way back?

Farewell clouds coming alive with bees.
Farewell firemen in the house.
Farewell deep flower-bruise of breath.
Farewell map's hum of apprehension and wheel of longing.

Farewell keeper's clockwise dance. . . all
Beginning comes ahead and backwards: of the aphrodisiac
After one has left: word memory
Which carries that scent, too sweet from the Phlox
Blossoms, blue gentians and yellow ranunculus. This, the search-flight
Where the wild swarm moves out
Like four points on a compass, is the beginning of the poem
From inside hive,—chronicle bloom, botanist's
            Finbos and tapestry,—to Queen of careless and care taking.

All at once, within the turnstyle consciousness, if
You let them, bees as words, strike like matches, flints to bone, striking
Back: maelstrom of directionless speech
First unleashed to the heart and that singular nectar in your ear
Whose invasion, translated by alarm and the scent organ, is
            Finally carried home.

Darwin's Window

> *A woman suffering from a brain damage disease was incapable of copying a square. When asked what these figures might mean, she replied, "the windows of a church." She did not draw squares without significance.*
> — Bruno Munari

She would not enter a room without windows, a church without
Angels. Trajectories will surpass disease. Ease
Without consideration, you figure as intervention here, to be here.

Vision, after all, since science, is physics; you are physics
When light praises light in the insect skin of leaves
When you look for the angels; when angels appear

In a square of paper, upon the pencil. She blinks. The windows
Open and close just like that, and without Michelangelo they lead
To other windows. Under the black wing umbrella of sleep, water falls

From her mouth onto her pillow: preempt dream. Sized to its fraction
She could draw a square around it, fit for windows, make more
Space to inhale the smallest dust, holy rising particles.

In a world's division, space means naming; a wasp curls into
A sweet pea and the planet is enlarged all over again outside
Her window. You sit across the room, out of order

And the unnatural selection of History stains the church glass
Above you both: glass-anonymous, glass-haunt, glass-us, glass
Of water and Darwin's earth colored ghost kneels below as if in

Overt reverence, with a pencil in one hand, the other full, closed on
Consideration, closed on the counted, colorless squares of broken glass.

Mother Tongue

We are all imperfect.
We are all derivative.
Made out of sugar and spice, pronoun-oath of faith, excess superlative
of lost love, predicate-salt of goodbye on the tongue
and therefore, the consequence of dictionary, every day
casualty of vocabulary.

Would I wear my words as hat to any other name?
Would I try on red for a change,
bind my breasts or bare my skin
to the schwa, one colorless vowel, the one phoneme
we slip into like a pair of old shoes?

Does my grammar make me gregal?
If I am gobemouche, then
the flies I have swallowed mock the hive
already made out of my words. Forbidding the logic

of happenstance, the honey, the look on my face
or leverage said by my body, you may understand me
before I say, sing, show my instrument of the deeper brain, rendering
itself once borrowed and broken
by a history of languages strung.

My motiloquent mood
makes me all beads and baubles, the glint
in someone else's blue eyes. My touch may make you mute.
I can moo and coo, I can covet. Make no bones

about it: these words keep making themselves
over in me. They are my marrow, chip
off the 'ol block, salt-lick, dice, flowers dissolving
upon my palms, and beginnings of self
self-defined but lost in definition.
Didn't you know? There is no finer art
unfinished. No plate left clean, no taste left

in the mouth to pursue on the pallet. My ingenuous
arch of triumph, my tightrope ass-walk, my dead
man's stare toward the 'right now,'—

This logology
is an excursion to your ear. It has its own case
of personal insomnia. It pronounces
what it can, of my feelings. Let's say it, now
trippingly on the tongue,
what drama was unleashed in the sky tonight.
Do I revive or relive the singular "I" ?
And what do I share in "we" ? Tongue-tied to a tease
of 'make me', or 'he made me do it.' Does the dress fit
the punishment? Does the reward outweigh
what we just ate?

My asparagus was once your sparrow grass.
Green birds flew from us.
We reaped the masculine wheat, feminine oats and neuter corn.
My muliebrity made me no weaker.
We eat cake and have caffeine and can't keep a straight sentence.
But, oh, sweet dicacity
scattering its pomegranate seeds over our bodies!

What I skelp and slurp, peel and make pearl
makes no difference
if you do or don't speak my mother tongue: what I make
is pure similitude of food, air, water, desire.
We all recognize our home, our homonym. So squeeze from me
what you can of Shakespeare's "breathing one's last breath"
and drive me to say just one more thing, let me

think about it further: we are all caught between
rack and ruin, vim and vigor, the first and foremost, between
what is safe and sound, seen and heard, what is null and void in the scheme
of life's beautiful redundancies. Let me get
one more word in, let one more animal out.
Do I make order out of chaos and dwarf the next context?
Change my appearance? See me as you say.

Look at me
when you say " I see what you mean."
Don't get me wrong:
I can mean what I say, seem
to say much more, or
with the wave of one hand over
the blank page of error, I can
say nothing at all.

In the Kingdom of Beetles

In the Age of Beetles
in Contradiction's Kingdom of More-Than, where millions
make up one of every four Earth animal species, they more than make up
for what we cannot see in front of us.
Chirruped, overlooked, spun in glass
by their own compounds: windows
to desert, forest floor, ice fields, the delicate
habitat of leaves and fur.
They resemble anything familiar: fortress, bird
droppings, boat and helicopter, bauble jewelry
or the most ancient Samurai shield.
Not one really the same.
Some blind, stilt-legged, armoured—scratched in air
with rasp and squeak, they share the rubbings of some other language.
So we shall find them first
from our imagination
and best, in our ignorance.
Among green-glowing mushroom gills, drawn to
ultraviolet light, underwater and atop a tropical white moth
or upon huge dung balls, incredulous to our design, taken up
to hitchhike on the mouthpart of bees, these beetles
once premiere pollinators, benevolent
and voracious predators, now store air, see
the underside, flee from the heat but multiply, fluoresce, multiply, shine
and divide the still uncounted.
All part of some great treasure
of confusion and beauty:
harlequin and dung, darkling, scarab, tortoise and rove and tiger—
Isn't beauty confusion after all, the sensation
of words lost in our bodies? No blandiloquence here.
Wittgenstein's "S" drops us like his Beetle in a Box
and leaves us there to be guessed upon: gleaming
ingot gold, ignited mosaic.
If my grammar had that kind of autonomy, then I would be
in a universe all my own
where beetles outnumber plants and inanimate

words are kept in a box.
Some of them “may be no longer than this sentence’s punctuation
marks,” no smaller than the opened wings
of sleep. Uniformly dull and iridescent paint
by number: this is our riddle, our distance, that
common ground of confusion
where our illiterate heads spin
like this full blue planet, and our hearts
beat and beat just a little bit faster.

Animalia

—for Galway

Ambivalence
can be a kind of animal, a kind of freedom.
Picture yourself
halfway to faith, covered in new feathers,
measuring the surrender
of sky, or phosphorescent in
scales changing color
when you belly the water.
In the kind of danger that makes you
over or transforms

inalienable will.
You are your own inconsolable
inspiration. You
wear the aftertaste of fruit
trees, stench of deer
as the wet grass lights up
along the ground ahead of you.

You have forgotten
your whereabouts but know
the night, deep in your black, your bear
fur. You can take
your time here.
So your mole feet dig
deeper for white root, your shining
mynah bird talks back inside of you
and the colonies of bees weave your hair:

all companion as animal to
yourself. The clarity of a lifetime
sleeps in your egg.

Every time you walk
out to the edge of the wind-arch
at this peninsula, the bird of prey in you
can see a solitary gray mouse dusting
the red dirt, only a mile away.

Paul Klee, Inexact Diaries

I never divide or reveal too little, I never know myself.
        You see, I am leaving memory's door, its distance behind.

I am the best kept secret beyond my name or hands;
            I make paintings. *Color*

Possesses me. I don't have to pursue it. Figures rise out of these
            Mixed numbers, intoxicated gardens, and this is

My work, untitled toward inseparable color. Clockwise
        Darkness pursues me in every storm.

That all along, I have been unfading here. As wing,
        Deliberation makes its own promise behind me.

I ask you nothing less of tight-rope air, territorial love, nourishment.
        I ask of you what a child knows, and more winter strength.

I say: *Do not frighten the nakedness in search of slumber,*
            Simplicity and shape, complicity and sleep.

What if only, I live here? Out of the cricket's heartbeat country I come.
        Down to the downpour of my being, and though I love words

And their wasp consonants, the coral oracles and all that
        Remains to the hard estimation of sound, I will return to

My physical self. *My head burns to the point of bursting. One*
        Of the worlds hidden in it wants to be born unbruised on a wish.

It's simple really, a way of life, one life on its long way,
            With paintings, to somewhere so inexact;

Despite any face and linen canvas opened, you needn't ask anyone
            Else. I wanted to be a poet. I should know. I was there.

Magritte's Hat

for me the world is a defiance of common sense.
—René Magritte

We wear it for prosperity, covet
the simple indiscretion, his surrealism. It is

our chair
when we want to be alone, bowl
for double-deck playing cards, chamber pot
or head challis. This is our *Key of Dreams*
where the error of language is ordinary; we pull
from the hat what we see.

We are nobody's fool.
This art knows us well.

This hat catches the carry
of wind to nowhere.
What universe isn't made of such circles?

What there is to love: life's hat, the self
we have given up against the grain.
And what dark do we have
to walk through again and again
without good sense?

Defiance is our bowler.
We can dismantle ourselves from the painting anytime,
wear what a stranger knows.
Redefine religion, take
what we need and keep ourselves intact.
Intact as the eye, over here. It begins
without color.

We know this, by collage and correlation.
We can fight tangible. After all,
we are human, on our way
home. We can follow ourselves, backwards,
and by heart. See: in the apple-sky

the hat just fits the face, holds enough
air for one more word.

God's Watch

The eighteenth century saw the universe as a watch wound by an omniscient watchmaker: God.
—Octavio Paz

With infinite tinkerings, spinning wheels, screws, needles
and pins of light, constant
motion, with the great sweeping precision
of one gesture held in air
against a clamoring key-note click and fitting
of this passive scheme, he sits
barefooted with a gold and black watch. God
speaks the word of watches, odd soliloquy:
God's password for omnipotence.
He takes the somnambulist's seat
next to the aisle of stars.
This is his ebullient ruin, the kind of detail
we cannot grasp.
Safe and clean-shaven, banal
and without a brain as we know it
between the divide of blackness and light: God.
Tell us something we don't know
about liars and art. Tell us something
about penumbra's mathematics. There is no hunger
in this kind of perfection and no appetite lost
to the consciousness. What may be random, ambiguous now,
carries the lock and key, coin of phrase
where the air is thin and without
a ladder to climb.
The Man and his watch burns
metaphysical matches
at the back of our heads down here. Up there, stars,
as God's braille for the back of his hands, for his animal skin,
shine like insistence. But toward that light
aging slows for Einstein's *clock paradox* where we never reach
destination, and to the grammar of good will to all men:
that injustice so vast, Time, heaven's
strong arm against us.

In Particular

Recognition in the body
moves like a swarm of bees: you know all
over at once. Your place
in history has not been betrayed
as you find what you really feel follows
no language: wild stir
of insects, flurry of birds, one bone
of the earth shows through, night root
                    tightened within its ground.
Can we be hypnotized by the primitive?
I heard a *tick, tick, tick*
once, turned and stared with the light
thinking about nothing.
But I noticed the fine grain of sink wood
like waves, weaving, the real bending
of trees against wind, over—how beautiful it was.
This is
what it is like before sudden disaster, before
the inhospitable truth:
our other brain, the one
which cannot speak, the one who sleeps incipient
on the job, walks the dog, erasure,
and gives in, hears
the *tick, tick, tick,* turns
toward it with the light
and makes us look—whether for the first
or last time, we look.

Answering Machine

Insatiable insomniac, sad
savior, art work worrying words
through the knitting needle eyes of silver wires;
its fish skinned cassette tape swims
around and around

the daydream's dizzy language
broken and asking completion. Relinquished
from responsibility, primogenitor
absolved from thought.

It is our teachers telling us
to work harder, the deeper past putting out
both hands for coins. Juke box gibberish,
electrical future guttural. A stranger
caught in the fingernail beep, that obscene
phone caller, dial tone addict, executor
of fast food chatter delivered.

Bodiless nevertheless, incorrigible
teller of tales and lies, disguised
excuses and kisses.
The echo of unremembered things, accidental
hollow drum's palindrome.

It is your unconsciousness
voicing its complaint or putting in
a good word for you; that someone you know,
still struggle to recognize. Perhaps
it is the black box body of God looking
out for you, saving some messages, cutting
other ones off, absorbing indiscreetly
your soul, stolen as you speak.

Take these
mechanics of the calendar missing a day,
rewind and fast forward intentions,
this quick erase of the heartbeat pattern
of the tongue. It might be
your father's silence
when he is alive, the white-wash of his voice
saying nothing.

So speak and be heard.
Hover your word or leave
a dial tone note because
keeping its own time, it holds vigil
with your voice, talking back to you;
in matters like these left behind, it is
the thing, the thing you can't ignore,
turned on, terrifying,
talking back to you.

Liberty As Warning

A state of chaos matters
as it forgets the body. A new language
is being made, take every word for it
from the voice, the black yap at the moon, the insatiable visitor
in the brain, flag bearer, gift horse and relentless
house guest. You know
what it feels like to rage till you are not afraid of anything
and the top of the sky is spinning
its icy waters at the top of your head.
Then something changes and you are in another country
of unanchored consideration.
There are velvet bugs there, bright birds let out, whole
generations of paintings. Look
for the clockwise spirit. Parasail out over the snow
with your socks on at night. Know its changed light. Beckon,
betray and begin again by talking in your sleep.
Somewhere there's always an opening. There is breath
and its several conciliatory directions.
How can you stop it? The unresolved walks on.
You walk on with a telescope, no
clothes, a silver thermometer and flowers
in your mouth. Silence,—
ok, someone to hold your hand. Your hand
free, but a way to find home.

III

Truth was the only daughter of Time. She once walked
the earth without clothes but her skin was occupied.
—Leonardo da Vinci

Pig's Eye

Idiomatic, those for granted idiosyncrasies, taken to heart.
"Pig's Eye!" father said with true authority. A favorite phrase
or set of swear words I never understood. Why the pig's eyes?
Surely, the pig had other body parts that would promise

a better insult, the afterlife of disturbance upon the one
it was said to. To what bristly hide, short tailed and to a point,
what mobile snout, cloven-hooved are we referring? He put his foot down.
"Certainly not," the dictionary reads. In other words, a final denial

to the brown eye of the pig whose circumference is the size of a button
on a man's business suit. Second son of a tree feller, my father the artist
on a farm of sorts, therefore knew his pigs well and our fondness
of disgust for them. Domesticated, greedy, obstinate animal

who knows the indignance of the future. I admit, I prefer animals
as a better part of the species of speech. What else could fall out
of the missing mouths of guardian angels and small children?
Who else could mix our metaphor, keep us warm at night?

Out of the parenthesis a daughter misses in her memory: parental cant, argot
of childhood, dialect of urge, consumer jargon, parlance paid for in advance,
and the simple act of a pig's eye upon you. I never really learned how to swear
right, but I can talk myself into a hole, man-made of course, and stand

my ground, a muddy one of sorts. From this thin air perspective, from
the sweet unequal word given, I am dragged that much closer to
Shakespeare, to the salty Earth, outweighed by all animals in our thinking
and so grateful for it. So, if I am deficient to believe the only insight

seen is the whale's gaze upon infinity, then I shall keep my eyes open, keep
my eye out for it when it comes: the perfect insult from the pig's swill
of words available. I am put to the sword, put to the task, to the tongue
every day because father made me part animal, one word at a time.

Immaculate Measure

The moon flips its coin in the deepened plot, black palm
of sky: one night mother-silver, tonight full father-gold

suspended there for my taking. I stand visible outside the hospital
under its universe-awning: scientists' relics, massive wisps

of primeval gas, Big Bang's night walk away from reasonable thinking.
I want to feel nothing, only this physical: wax-star and night-beetle

night's drum, the leaden ax of cold air hard down and the earth's center
candle wick still red, that great gravitational plow-pull forward

from sky to sky, or the roister of dawn's birds, then wind raising
its cut glass arms over these hills...and the physical

of my father, carved permanent as parents are in perfect
shape, burned-in smell and familial color; the orbital curve

of father's head, the part of him I want to touch most, framed
there, floats from its white pillow for my hands.

So, when I think he is going to die, when I believe the bed
in the hospital will too become his other body

I resist the whole of him, placed where we all started
from, as one powerful dot, distanced and centered at the end

of each morning's period typed out, now
pore, pinhead, bed mite, one exhaled atom

and as I see it, reversed immaculate power
above me, slow galaxy, the child's father, father-time

father-heaven, father-order, perhaps retreating back
into his revisionist's tempest, my father emerging

for air, nominal, inexact of these sciences, just there
to turn his face toward me again.

Without the Elation of Rage

The light shines in the darkness...
The word became flesh and made his dwelling among us.

Body of rain
body of water
body of God from the words:
body of my father.
Lying in his final weightlessness
of words, lighter
in the floating bed
of blue weeds, fire-clouds,
dreaming in the beginning
where there was once the working
hard flesh of my father
painless and shining
in the darkness as the planets
do, as God must have done
in the minds of those
who wanted him to.
But today is another
day of rest for my father
who has no reprieve
from his body, its slow temblor;
what hurts the earth's reddened core
hurts first language
and the standard of hours
as they blow against
his white surrender flags of breath.
What makes for Glory
and full of Truth remains
dust in his draftsman's hands,
on the palate and tongue
and so buried in the ash of my voice
dusting over him.
I keep what I say simple.
I drive the steel train of my rage

backwards, become soft,
a similitude of silence. Father,
I am here to touch you, to remind
us both we are fleshing-out
the words and their moon-faced
contexts, each one
dissolving every evening
like the Host on the sky,
the black tongue of God.

Thirst for Them

Carry the lost faces
with you, those clockworked
beneath the ground, thirsty as blue
earthenware, as desire, as inked destination
of their memory. Count them
              with the number of hours
it takes to make a day. The dead
are necessary for living:
they are the digits between your bones,
carpet threads clung
to your shoes in the closet.
Every exhale and disposition of used air, now
numb ambition of everything human
though you can still feel them
in the animal heat. Feel them
in your sleep
out of the duplicate darkness
and plural air. Persistent
              as consequence, they make memory,
together, with us, the strange order
of another morning. Make what you will
of yourself with them, carry them, carry
their salt-lick distances
with you.
Whatever it will take
in the rousal of leaves from making
light, in the first bird's feet
leaving the branch,—and what
it may take from you to wake
and wake and wake
again, each day, to need
them, thirst
for them, whoever they are
who need you.

Breaking Unbalance

Elegy for Lynne

I

The immense lungs of the sky
darken and damage, each tree
coughing up the iodine cold, and further
down below, our family
stands together to say goodbye: you step out
under the factual house lights walking
the body's reticence, backwards
each step, across the wet lawn.

II

From a breaking unbalance above,
with the weight of waxen fruits: the rain
comes hard and shining, silver
tea leaves brailled, clinging
against these shut blackboard windows.
All night the rain
carries away whole islands
of roiled debris, ankle-deep down
the street. To set
myself back on the heel of darkness,
I slide the clock under my pillow
to keep quiet, feel its ticking in my teeth—
your children, now sleeping next to me—all
of us, all else, of all less, it is all
we can do here waiting.

III

But I can also hear
the water in my sleep, the incessant
clapping, softened storm-applause
as if you were stirring yourself
out of the dark
toward us, as if all of us knew
remembrance before loss, understood
the anatomy of your disappearance—like an actor
who gathers what he can of himself
before leaving the stage—you are
even more like the water, still leaving. . .

IV

We know now, ruing against
the injustice of logic, how
it happened: too much like this
image under water, your hair
attending new shapes in black and white
between the trees; where
the river rose, the turned canyon's
red road washed away your car, where you
last let go of breathing:

V

Here, the street glances back up
at us, polished by the downpour
like a black patent leather shoe
bearing the terrible weight of God
against you; revised rhymer
of water passing from sky to land to lungs—
joint creator revoking
your errand home; this deviant loss
we share as our own.

VI

We don't need a picture
to picture you now: a difference
of weather between us, parable
hours counted out loud
before the street lamp's dim
prophesying your death
at dusk, that awful knowing we feel
before we are pulled by
the star's peripheral dark
locked down here—enough

water memory to keep us
swimming, mouth to mouth
standard touching, hands rising up
to your solvent face flashing its candle, and no one
strong enough to pull you
from our sides.

Childhood

It's difficult to tell the truth, since there is only one truth,
but that truth is alive and therefore has a lively, changing face.
—Franz Kafka

I

The sun is a lively faceless paper coin, silver
above the trees.   Our neighbor is watering her yard
and its tidy rows of uncertainty: deep purple azalea & hydrangea.
I wish my hands into the air for stray drops. A double blue appears:
her eyelids and the deep breath of sky.
I am nine years old, looking
for lizards between the broken cracks in the house.
I am looking for anything: mailman, worm, little tooth, toys,
what must be mistaken about the lost past. I am looking
for my sister who is alive.   There is no province
of what is important: without the body, live air and no wager
at all.

II

The sun is an exhale, changing behind the gray insomnia
of clouds.   Our neighbor will not water her yard
and its untidy rows of certainty: pale green weed, eucalyptus.
My hands press the dry air's flat glass. Nothing
appears, nothing answers back.
I am nine years old, looking
for what must be mistaken about the lost future,
for the unbroken face of our house, for the nothing of the particular
and what finds you: grass & ants, the smell of paint, dirt.
I am looking for the distance in dream, ghost-incoherence, looking
for my sister who is not alive.   There is a province
of importance: between the body, still air and the wager
for it all.

Without Exception

...Yet we do after all
Belong here, and have moved a considerable
Distance; our passing is a facade.
But our understanding of it is justified.
—John Ashbery

The truth is always wasted on what we know.
Here we are, instrument to less than what we believe, elsewhere.
The deepest ocean answers its blue phone over and over and everyday risk
Remains a walk in the dark as yesterday for the child, without exception,
Who recalls one cloud above Rome light up cantaloupe, her love
Like all the figures of speech, now left behind and opposing.

We are not part of the public persuasion, domain of fear opposing
Our company together, nor Rorschach canvas. What we do know:
Picturing the the deep hurt that is winter's earth, lasting one love
Between mother and daughter, this profound language of the senses elsewhere
In our bodies. We are the inimical music of the universe, an exception
To the rule, without exception, as if our life depended on this last risk.

I am not your deaf ear cauliflowered white, to the ground, every risk
You ever wanted to take. You are not my hammer in the water opposing
Gravity and regret. Time takes its own simple exception
And decides which dream of bees, which music we hear and know
Until we have rocked ourselves back to sleep, deep, elsewhere
In the exhumed grave of the brain seeking new pennate light: love.

Until, unalterable, we grant farewell fails no real love.
Until the painting's pure argument is parting, change without risk.
Until each wave's leap from the heart knows what it is opposing.
Until the thimbles of the dead fill with rain, keep their dwelling elsewhere.
Until the barehanded conductor brings the rust train to a stop we know.
Until the doctor heals each umbrella's broken rib, cures the exception.

And you and I return the salt to its gate-water, take exception.
And the trees are filled with the vigil of birds, exceeded by love.
And our bones are given back to the fire, full ache of knowing.
And all the uneasy blossoms precede falling, decide their risk.
And you and I break our cups, believe in nothing else opposing.
And the last fishing boats light the creosote distance elsewhere.

Because we can do nothing else disproportionate at home, elsewhere
When the very thing we could not predict was our exception
When the melancholy animal met its black match, opposing.
Because like it or not, we threaded the dull needle of language against love.
Because we are nothing less than the wedge in the floorboards: lost risk.
Because I am afraid of nothing but your flowered lack of knowing

For it will bring us to our thin husks and the opposing
Will of knowing when to die and live, when, in final love,
To take the exception of risk with us into the brutal, wild elsewhere.

Every Definitive in July

The weather has beaten us
Down again; we are only animal, insect.
Moths cling to the screens outside
Like tiny flags pinned to a land map.
Our survival's not fit for what we have
In mind of giving up our shoes, solemn
Talks. Time has taken up all the air. There
Must be more ahead, more than these
Empty water jug clouds leading us
Toward thirst. Today will be like any other
Tomorrow. Perhaps this is just
An annunciation in wandering: the feel
Of miles of beach under our feet. See: those
Fevered waves at a distance are overwhelmed
By their own history. No one
Will walk on this water.

Mutiny Allegory

To the wood floor of the boat
water makes pattern and dries: salt water, unrecognizable flower
the sea and its fragile company
where we navigate, even have time to watch, by the inevitable return
of its icy waves, this ocean
which throws up disguise, white caps, its self regard and a hard view,
pure dereliction.
Queen of the bow, I, maiden-head, see you with pirate patch
and a yell to match it, pace.
The sun might as well be thrown ice and gets in the way.
My hair gets in the way
but I know I have always taken this voyage by storm, taken it
with you. Only
this time there has been a shift of liberty and no life boat above
water, this water
which is luxury: its frames close and open black, magenta, green and blue,
invite me to leave without you,
willful, torn invitation, to loose memory and scout for a severed island because
since chance and the long voyage
home, the crew fell overboard, the mast lost its sail in the last gust,
not a bird in sight, and if
you think about it, the horizon is crooked, the natives, unfriendly.

Of Angels & Loneliness

Were I to arrive
with wet earth, my hair, in that other
invented heaven
where angels & loneliness live, I would
press my tongue hard, to the cleft in your chin
so as to hear the small green cricket sing
            at the base of my spine.

But singing has been singled out
for us, separate and safe from this. We part
with words, keep recognition of each other
incendiary and alive
in language where its little black ash feathers
float, where its havoc can play muse, where
our hands guide the dark as worship
            to what we do not know.

We cannot forecast the future
of desire, walk the rough plank in a storm, feed
the flying fish or even hunger after ourselves.
At times like these, we raise
the drawbridge, batton-down the hatches, keep house
in the mind and in the mind's other room
            in the body: the sex.

Where skin is bewildered by joy,
where melancholy is the animal-ache
of personal mystery, we see each other, face to face
in the promiscuous & benevolent air of dream, wearing
water, bedside manners and the prayers of kisses
            along our ribs.

We see what we want to say; we save
our loneliness. As rain's spendage, fire's devour, the stars'
flash of bone, what are we really ripened from?
Would I inhabit surrender to you there, shape imagination

as an orange, whole in my palm, peel
its scaled oil-skin, lift a wedge to the roof of the mouth
with my tongue—this worshiping, every day answer
        to a simple question—

then, I would still be alone. But we bring
our reluctant sincerity to the greenhouse, god house
the halfway house, to the whorehouse. Twin accidents
in discipline, already disciples of each other's passion.
A live Tamarind seed cast from a tree, bee's wings, millions of them
gathered with dawn, make up a phantom religion, a portent-place
where we won't lay ourselves down to breathe the relentless free air
        and sweeter smell of each other.

Bee's Connubial Hive

is where I press my head
center into your chest precisely as if

to hear your voice, erotic earwig,
sexual organ for my tragus-need, as if

to hear you vowel and swerve
into zero's solemn unlimited

O, is climax enough.
I make my bearings by

your word, the flesh's past-time
transformation, hive's groin-spot

of humming into a golden
conundrum slowed here

multiplied by your breath there,
twice the dizzy drug of pause

until that magnetic cloud
remains my nubile

and billows all over me
like an act of God

or an act of dominioned weather
where I would roll with you

and the sweet pornographic aspect
of your voice, forever.

Red Pillow

Flammable curtains and chairs, French around her, estrangement
became a kind of fatigue—fatigue, the gods' belated impatience by her
costume, silks from boats in second light, remains now her embroidered
pleasure and what she once claimed each time he left. Left intention
makes its own promise. Promise stitched by stitch to a thread count
and deep red. Deep red, she wore the future's reticence but believed in the past's
ambiguous hunger: hunger and lust by surprise is always
a simple fiction at first. First invested bloom, her fruit's taste became how good
his incongruity was, his desires were. Were the orchard's
ceiling a glass tune, then birds doubled in song. Song and tongue-silk combined by
red, their two lives made uncertain alliances. Alliances
were weak because they were made out of love. Out of love, she had worn this red
to his double flame, its deep vermian vermilion, its one shine
patterned from single regard. Regard's slow cure, she would waste no time
between her hands or words tracing the darker gold
now nearly gray brocade with her smallest finger, a skin map. A skin map
drawn, he observed her center. Center, away from herself

even in sleep. Sleep and the handmaiden's hard work, hours of her restlessness
worn, caught perfection through the needle's foreign eye, a weave
in waves. In waves by then, without control, the rain took the red dirt roads and
green ocean between them. Between them, what cloth ransom would
he make to make her believe they were where they belonged, and what other way
was there to know himself beyond her boundaries? Boundaries
were drawn over conjecture's surrender in a season beginning without consent
Consent over his sexual fires' establishments for the once unclaimed, once
departed, now a deliberate loss of memory. Memory, if by the oyster-hour's end of each
stitch belonged to these two, if not sped, a love, beyond quick
judgment before her, her riches and father gone, lost by sea, one father ago—then
memory would feel alive. Alive, one father ago, his father there laid down
hemp words of money against her. Against her transparency, she came to be strong
by this and worn opaque with such fate. Fate's invitation is silent.

Silent, she made no more wish for herself, now held by doubt's vowels though
the gown bore last resemblance undone, of her desire unmade.
Unmade by no one, she would fall over her own days, make herself a body's
grievance upon him. Upon him, she would weigh the red and its maze

of roses, she would raise his lust's conceit and season, trust gone. Gone, left behind,
        her gown's hem in a pillow for him, the hourless red in pieces, this
stound sewn to his sleep, taken and returned beyond night and its kelp ties: no
        sexual rose to know, no flower's head left, no maiden voyages, carved tables
with song. With song bewildering by desire, she would lie down in an open canoe, his
        canoe, dark filled with red flowers and set out to sea. Sea and a simple
drug, sound of water's lift, gust and drift and the last threads of birds unstitching
        the sky's dry panel, one silver thimble over each finger, candle red wax seal
set on each palm, each palm death-opened over her breast, red's wasted lasting rare
        radiance wasted on red. Red pillow, umbilical fire, fire stitch taken from
the heart-gut, burned out, now and forever, for him as companion, a new stranger.

Red

From the head of a rose
scattered drift to our bed: bright
curved tongues. We have broken our speech. We sleep
over the ones that darken and stick to our skin: one
on the eyelid, between buttocks, lips, each nipple, flush
as a kiss in the ear where spring opens out
and answers no one. Each red
of the rose has been rubbed into the white sheet,
fire-stained and darkened, extinguished
as a bruise. We live here
in a lack of time. We shall sex flowers, feel
them fall from the neck, rosary-aviary
in scarlet flight. These rushed kisses
pressed in burn and burnish, as if
peeled from the skin:
slow lick, slow curse
over the heart, undiminished
by its own stain. We look
into the eyes, we look into the brain.
Admit: *flower, flower, flower.*

Palm

These palms could withstand
the slight weight shift of my hips
as I lower over you
in a lavender rhythm of breathing.
They could pad my back,
be the blindfolded
tour guides of my legs.
These palms could lift me
from the entanglement of minutes.
Palms that could carry
just enough water
for us to drink, that could unharm
raspberries and cover each ear
or mouth, the forehead's bare agenda,
pubic bone's endearment—your palms
like bird bellies, sex
before it happens, the wordless
place we move into—held
out over my sleep, cusped
like a first bra
over my breasts in an imaginary
wish for naming all
body parts. I unpeel
your hands close to my face,
each finger half-closed, feel
your palms as though they were
small animals unraveling sleep
and separate from your body.
Knowledge comes from this: palms
held open like a book
to be read in the dark. Their tributaries
unfollowed, the life lines
unended from here.
The palm is the bed. The palm
never sleeps.

To Bird

The Dutch word volgehen *means "to bird" and "to copulate."*

I wake up, under you, unfold,
                    unfold and unfold.
Everything is wing: hand, hip & cheek.
Everything is motion, each other's.
In the high favor of the wind, blue weakness and gone
                    from the nest, feathered and falling
fast, I burn by weightlessness toward you.
Bird-nest, bird-breast
                    in your whole hand.
By bird passage, caught in the hollow bone wheel
of our inaudible domain,
we reshape drift, reshape dive and hover, we follow
the body's great distances and close in:
breathe, breathe. . .
nipple against the tip of your cock,
                    my hair and your thumb in
my mouth, refusing nothing. We bird
and bird, glad from up here, to be
begging for our lives,
grateful again, to be almost
                    air.

Watermark

Your mouth loses what it is going to say, the trajectory
of consciousness. Without warning
from my body first, a wild kiss unfolds
toward your mouth. Each kiss
at a time, I lose the minutes,
release and taste
you, press, breathe backwards,
billow and purse.

So I open your lips, each one,
a cushion for breath, each one,
hem of the world, this aspiration
and tongue I envelop
without knowledge of future or past. Erase
and release everything sweetly: meridian
crossed, small talk, borrowed word
long vowel
of my being here, opened
wet oracle and hallucinatory search
for the beginning of you
in my body. Oh, faithful taste, we can eat
of each other. We can offer everything
of nothing more than this: a kiss
of mangoes washed
from the sea or loose seeds
in an unattended field, planted and retrieved.

So I open the mouth of this kimono
printed with mango
birds, open the bird cage of your mouth, this
small aviary for an oath of folded breath, for an oath
of folded light, for the birds we plume into each other, flown
first from the ribcage
where bird is that figure for breath
where we inhale
again and again to catch the first syllable

of lust, unfixed approval of the self handed over
to another, in a kiss, where we might break the spell of our names
language's lost itinerary,—
kiss the sleep awake
withhold our slipped logic and speak
for imperfection's sake

making no separation
between this kiss
between what has been lost
and left behind
falling forward from consideration
propelled toward the bird-dark
spinning out innumerable other kisses
like spun wheat pulled from the fields of Arles
where we exhale our hunger
at last: sheer human watermark
into fresh air. . .

The Future Comes to Him, Faithless: A Dialogue

Maybe you're the future
and who lives there, the command of language,
flesh's unstoppable bloom in a fever's sway-cancellation of the hours,
maybe you're absent from the hours set before you
so you can always have the last word.

—she said.

> *Your own persuasion has you again, doesn't it?*
> *Look: is it the first picture you make with your hands,*
> *the one you hold up to your face that you recognize, but tell me,*
> *who do you recognize?*
>
> —he makes his way to the chair,
>
> *Not hunger's closed fist opening out of the intellect,*
> *a peppered flower, no, not the rain dissolving away*
> *all rational absolutes or the green weight of feeling, no,*
> *no, say your name to me, to the lips without discretion, close*
> *to the heart-wasp. . .*

As if you could begin again
ahead of yourself, as if you know who you are.
The hours are set before you, the full porcelain plate of minutes
and you will not move, will you? You won't make a move.
As if I could slow you down to have a good look, anticipatory to
what you have always looked for: on the wall,
mirror, mirror. Not me.

—she doesn't have to see him standing.

> *There is no better chaos than this. I too have hunger*
> *for a lack of perfection, the disarray of stars, understanding*
> *of the odds and it held me once in its husks, the hourglass of August*
> *and the heat, until I couldn't think. Prove me wrong. We are*
> *easily equal to one lie, aren't we? And you, sweet apparition, giving up*
> *the air around you, but not a dime of perfection?*
>
> —he raised his hands as if in surrender.

IV

I must keep 'gas' burning to light the danger up,
so I could distinguish it— these gave me a snarl
in the brain which don't unravel yet, and that old
nail in my breast pricked me.
—Emily Dickinson

Copernican Revision: The Flammable Bird

"Let it in truth guide the circling family of planets. . ."
guide the family of languages.
Let it in truth be an argument of light, the flammable bird, little
bit of habit you prove yourself upon

until you are object and you are spinning,
merry-go-round in the middle.

Heliocentric, centered away from yourself, moons
and elliptical orbits
wind, with dizzy view of the heavens
blinking above, this universe
of masterpiece giving what *Little Commentary*
you leave behind.

You are this taste of mathematics,
all heat and injury, once
heretic and hungry, so what is left
to divide and conquer?
Darkness disassembling desire
where yearning is your proceeding
there

one planet away from the center, and you are the present tense
mystical talk of the future
the changing faith
of a few thousand years, long ago in the Kingdom of Seeing
where, light years away, after retrograde
motion, after implosions' colored bands
of gas spiraled, you were
the center of a Black Hole so dense
you could not be weighed against the Gods;
your head could not be lifted
from the pillow.

Detail in Black

for Agha Shahid Ali

You said the dark cannot be touched during this time of year,
wrenched from itself or you, this Pacific sea and sky trench
opened. We stand in the doorway motionless, whether to let the light

out or smell of the sea in, to watch one fishing boat rock and cut
its figure from the lack of horizon, scatter its anchovy net
of pinched light upon the water. Now we are this task of becoming

by insight, a sudden disturbance of birds, their winged
and white carphology with the light keeping us up late. Further
away from home, we startle what we know from within

each other's lost vernacular, in this moment, caught under
the fish skin water we cannot see, by phosphorescence's
green attention and, caught also, on the lip of each wake there

where, if we had our inhuman way, we would
ride and tease the candle of every bird flickering
till our hands were occasions of black and green and white

above our heads, and every hour was a dizzy undulant
of withheld words and invented delight for each other.
The ocean huffs and puffs and blows all its houses down

though we cannot see it. Fishermen pull their fish
out of winter's black mouth, this inner air's oracle
concealed, and we let it happen, swallow us whole

as if the world was nothing else but an unhinged wreckage of birds
and light troubling faith's finite kingdom of thirst, continent's
ghosting for fish and our every day earned lack of attention to Time.

Field of Aphasia

Nature herself has no grammar.
—Fenollosa

Speech was always consequence
once, consciousness. With a rowboat full of rocks,
a man is determined to make it to shore:
the wind rocks him.
Bubbles and salt water release
between hairy lips of black mussel shells
corked alongside the bench-fitted, capsized shelved rock
of these tide pools, now alive
with animate hiss and spit.

As though human
vowel or consonant, an aqueous alphabet
choired its own impact, dropping
shoes, rice colored bones, fingernail-chips of shells
shining from an entanglement, still green, indiscriminate:
this ocean's exhale.   By the heat, by not a single word
overhead, clouds
float, premonitioned by the last sun
and their vaporous colorings fire up all at once
like the Deity brain synapsed in the dark.
Fire coral, antique blue.
I rub the sand into my skin.
What primitive privilege
from silence is this? Backwards,
the man
in the wooden boat, returns, drops
two tongues, oars,
down into the throat of the water.

Going after Shakespeare

to beggar all description, anything you want, easily equal
to the art of one lie, and just ask for one more kiss, for lack of
perfection, Rembrandt's face
from the orange-peeled darkness, pitch
black where you can hear the snow's dry sound
of porch light moths caught
under your feet, or as far out as you can go, deep
into the salt water, neck high, parting your hair where
blue stars are thrown like dimes, understanding
the odds, the limit of zero, bottomless disbelief
where God has a mathematical desire
not to be known, where you look right through
the empty sleeve of thought, through
the downdraft-sky hurling its white feathers of light, here
and here between memory's lost hemisphere
and the mind's tiny watch needles set down
into the body's water, never to come back, woo or speak
for you, nothing as easy as that, nothing flush
from this dark, fleshed out or feeding
on you, no, no chaos better than this, this astonishing
translation, gray carrier pigeon or thrown pack of cards, this
early graft of pear, dear anise flower and goat milk
to devour, this heart running its drunken numerals, sex
drive or devotional command, unresolved desire
sent adrift at the bottom of a canoe, or you
stirring yourself at the bottom of the black kettle,
becoming the unrolled blank canvas, the full clothesline
swinging in your sleep where everyone breaks
the bread of deep dream,
opens the fruit cage, throws
tangerine peels to the feet, holds out both hands
where everything becomes curiosity,
a light bulb swallowed whole, your lost suitcase opened, or
guess at it, your last chance, your random perfection's last
good word, way with me, your word, your ghost dissolved
as an unfixed chip of the universe, deed undone, passing

the buck, the dropped stone of my name,
holding out both hands and asking,
always asking,
from me, for more of myself
than I can ever give to myself.

Notes

In "Sanctuary of Hunger," "necessary irrepressible" is taken from Rainer Maria Rilke's *Letters on Cezanne*, his letter to Clara, Paris VIe, 29, rue Cassette, Monday, June 24, 1907. Rilke unfolds one of his own liberties of communication, telling us, "Surely all art is the result of one's having been in danger, of having gone through an experience all the way to the end. . .and the thing one is making is, finally, the necessary, irrepressible, and, as nearly as possible, definitive utterance of this singularity." I deliberately removed the comma that separates necessary from irrepressible so that, in this context, irrepressible may function as a noun.

"Porcelain": The word for the types of earthenware or china came into English via French, from Italian *porcellana* 'cowrie shell,' referring to the ware's shell-like finish. The word for the shell, in turn, is an adjectival form of *porcella*, a diminutive of porca, 'sow.' This came about because the shell was thought to resemble the vulva of a pig.

"Ghost: A Love Story": Growing up with artists, I found that everything revealed a visual and physical property, a primitive kind of separate existence. Therefore, vowel and consonant could be easily personified. This is one of those marvelous errors of perception.

"The Mother Tongue" is based, in part, on the orientation of consciousness made by language; the constraints not only multiply meaning, but seem to engender what Heather McHugh (*Broken English: Poetry and Partiality*) calls the "missingness. . .the missing before something's seen, and the missing after." This gets even more interesting if "you think you know yourself, [and] you haven't looked far enough into that distance where your strangeness is." Thank you, *Mrs. Byrne's Dictionary of Unusual, Obscure, and Preposterous Words*.

"In The Kingdom Of Beetles": *National Geographic*'s detailed images relinquish one's ignorance to one's imagination, the other kind of understanding; Wittgenstein declares, in his *Philosophical Investigations*, "Now someone tells me that he knows what pain is only from his own case! — Suppose everyone had a box with something in it: we call it a 'beetle'. No one can look into anyone else's box, and everyone says he knows what a beetle is only by looking at his beetle. — Here it would be quite possible for everyone to have something different in his box. One might even imagine such a thing constantly changing. —But suppose the word 'beetle' had a use in these people's language? —If so it would not be used as the name of a thing."

"Red Pillow"'s conceit developed from a close study of an all-red pillow made from Victorian ribbons. Using the anaphoric type lines, taking the last word or words from a sentence to begin the next, I found the narrative writing itself, red, as the eye of the storm, though the setting imagined became more 17th century in its formality.

"Detail in Black" was my first poem written for the brilliant, lovely Agha Shahid Ali. Shahid and I fell in love the moment we met. On one of his reading visits to Los Angeles we spent the day and night together; he offered to cook an authentic Indian meal which was far, far more extraordinary than I anticipated. Years later, before he was ill, Shahid sent me a copy of his poem, " The Purse-Seiner Atlantis" (*Rooms Are Never Finished*), inspired by our experience; we saw two things that night: a startling phosphorescent tide lighting up the frothy heads of waves and one anchovy fishing boat, hovering at a distance, in the blackness. The experience, the poem, now feels elegiac by nature. To quote Bob Hass in his interview with Bill Moyer: "There is a buried metaphorical pun in the Japanese that all Buddhist teaching is rooted in: All being awake is saying good-bye. Or, to put it another way, every time we say good-bye, we awake to the nature of things."